A  LITTLE  BOOK  OF  CELTIC  PRAYER

# A LITTLE BOOK
# OF CELTIC PRAYER

*A daily companion and guide*

COMPILED BY ANTHONY DUNCAN

Marshall Pickering
*An Imprint of* HarperCollins*Publishers*

Marshall Pickering is an Imprint of
HarperCollins*Religious*
Part of HarperCollins*Publishers*
77–85 Fulham Palace Road, London W6 8JB

First published in Great Britain in 1996 by Marshall Pickering

1 3 5 7 9 10 8 6 4 2

A catalogue record for this book is
available from the British Library

0 551 03052 6

Printed and bound in Great Britain by
Woolnough Bookbinding Limited, Irthlingborough, Northamptonshire

# CONTENTS

# INTRODUCTION

## The Character of Celtic Spirituality

Perhaps the greatest single calamity to overtake Western Christianity in recent centuries has been the divorce of the head from the heart and the exaltation of the former over the latter. In large part, this is a product of the Renaissance, translated into religious terms by the cataclysmic upheavals of the Reformation.

During this period, in reaction against superstition – real and supposed – reason was exalted and intuition was discounted, even feared and denied. In this climate, religion became to a very large degree head-centred rather than heart-centred, and Sunday religion began, slowly and inexorably, to part company with the religion of the hearth. We, in our generation, are the inheritors of the fruits of this troubled period.

Celtic spirituality, as we are now rediscovering it, is the religion of the hearth. It is also the religion of what, in terms more familiar to our Orthodox brethren, we might describe as 'the mind in the heart'.

There is no flight from reason in Celtic spirituality; very far from it. Nor is there any flight from intuition either. The Celt is above all a realist. Poet he may be – he may choose to define himself more naturally in terms of myth than in those of history, a profoundly valid thing to do – but there is none of the 'Celtic Twilight' about the Celt! His feet are on the ground, and very firmly set.

Celtic spirituality is deeply Trinitarian. In addition, it presupposes a wholeness within which there is no possibility of separation between the farmer, his cow, the saints in heaven, the holy angels, the mother of God and the ever-loving Triune Creator.

The beauty of nature is always a reflection – even an icon – of its Creator. There is no conceivable distinction made between 'religion' and 'life'. Life is lived in the unselfconscious and utterly natural relationship of beloved creature and beloved Creator, and in company with all other beloved creatures in Heaven and upon Earth.

The voice and tone of Welsh spirituality is subtly different from that of Gaelic-speaking Scotland and Ireland, but it is the same vision, the same deeply biblical, profoundly Christian understanding and tradition. It might be said to owe less – perhaps a great deal less – to the churches and chapels of recent centuries than to the monasteries of Derry and Iona, and to the spirituality of a Wales which resisted acceptance of the authority of Canterbury until the very last years of the twelfth century.

Most of all, perhaps, it was the embattled and ever endangered Celtic languages themselves that enshrined this ancient and blessed tradition. Impenetrable to the Anglo-Saxon, and all too often proscribed, the ancient languages articulated the Celtic Christian vision to perfection. In our own day they have yielded to translation; this remarkable heritage of wholeness is now made available to others who have lost too much of their innocence, their imagination, their vision and even, sometimes, their faith.

## The Arrangement of the Book

The material is arranged, following a generally consistent pattern, in seven chapters corresponding to the seven days of the week. Celtic spirituality is about life and the living of it, and so this arrangement suggested itself as ideally suitable for the whole character of the material. Spirituality is a living thing; as soon as it becomes academic it dies!

Each day carries its traditional dedication to a mystery of the faith, although the material does not always relate specifically to it, for life is lived in its totality in the context of the whole mystery of the love of God.

It is hoped that this book will be of use for daily devotional reading and meditation. Each day is divided into sections for morning, midday, evening and night, in order to make the book more readily accessible. However the book is used, deepening familiarity with this part of our devotional heritage reveals 'religion' to be life, lived in the context of the eternal love affair. The whole of creation begins, once more, to reveal itself to us as the transfigured image of its Creator.

ANTHONY DUNCAN

NORTHUMBERLAND, 1996

# Sources

Everything included in this anthology, save for one or two items, is translated from an original in one of the Celtic languages. Perhaps the most important single source is that astonishing life's work of the late Alexander Carmichael known as the *Carmina Gadelica*, or *Ortha nan Gaidheal*. This massive, six-volume work in both Gaelic and English translations, exhaustively annotated, represents the work of a lifetime spent collecting the oral traditions of prayers, charms, blessings and customs of the Gaelic speakers who inhabited the West coast and Isles of Scotland in the nineteenth century. The initials *CG* after an extract indicate that it comes from the *Carmina Gadelica*. Full references to the exact volume each such extract comes from are listed in the acknowledgements on pages 134–137.

The Welsh publishers, Gomer, have produced a small treasury of Welsh language works in translation. Among them is the remarkable *A Welsh Pilgrim's Manual*, in both languages, from which I have been happy to discover gem after gem for inclusion in these pages. The thoughtful and scholarly work of Patrick Thomas in *Candle in the Darkness*, from the same publisher, was also an inspiration.

K. H. Jackson's translations of Celtic originals are well known and his *A Celtic Miscellany* has contributed substantially to this work.

The poet Euros Bowen, a priest of the Church in Wales, wrote in his native Welsh and translated some poems himself into English. Others have continued this good work and Bowen's very distinctive and very Celtic vision is also to be found herein. There are others, including a hitherto unpublished poem by M. T. Harris.

# 1 ◉ SUNDAY

*The first day of the week; the Resurrection;*
*the first day of the new creation.*

## Morning

### THE GUIDING LIGHT OF ETERNITY

O God, who broughtst me from the rest of last night
Unto the joyous light of this day,
Be Thou bringing me from the new light of this day
Unto the guiding light of eternity.

    Oh! from the new light of this day
    Unto the guiding light of eternity.
    CG

# THE CROSS OF THE SAINTS AND THE ANGELS

The cross of the saints and of the angels with me
From the top of my face to the edge of my soles.

O Michael mild, O Mary of glory,
O gentle Bride of the locks of Gold,
Preserve ye me in the weakly body,
The three preserve me on the just path.
>    Oh! three preserve me on the just path.

Preserve ye me in the soul-shrine poor,
Preserve ye me, and I so weak and naked,
Preserve ye me without offence on the way,
The preservation of the three upon me to-night.
>    Oh! the three to shield me to-night.

CG

### Thought for the Day
*Am fear nach seall roimhe seallaidh e 'na dhéigh.*

The one who does not look forward will look back.

## *Daily Household Duties*

## KINDLING THE FIRE

I will raise the hearth-fire
As Mary would.
The encirclement of Bride and of Mary
On the fire, and on the floor,
And on the household all.

Who are they on the bare floor?
John and Peter and Paul.
Who are they by my bed?
The lovely Bride and her Fosterling.
Who are those watching over my sleep?
The fair loving Mary and her Lamb.
Who is that anear me?
The King of the sun, He himself it is.
Who is that at the back of my head?
The Son of Life without beginning, without time.

   CG

# MILKING CROON

Come, Brendan, from the ocean,
Come, Ternan, most potent of men,
Come, Michael valiant, down
And propitiate to me the cow of my joy.
    Ho my heifer, ho heifer of my love,
    Ho my heifer, ho heifer of my love.
    My beloved heifer, choice cow of every shieling,[1]
    For the sake of the High King, take to thy calf.

Come, beloved Colum of the fold,
Come, great Bride of the flocks,
Come, fair Mary from the cloud,
And propitiate to me the cow of my love.
    Ho my heifer, ho heifer of my love.

The stock-dove will come from the wood,
The tusk will come from the wave,
The fox will come but not with wiles,
To hail my cow of virtues.
    Ho my heifer, ho heifer of my love.
    CG

1.    sheiling: summer pasture.

# HYMN OF THE SUNDAY

On the holy Sunday of thy God
Give thou thine heart to all mankind,
To thy father and thy mother loving,
Beyond any person or thing in the world.

Do not covet large or small,
Do not despise weakling or poor,
Semblance of evil allow not near thee,
Never give nor earn thou shame.

The ten commands God gave thee,
Understand them early and prove,
Believe direct in the King of the elements,
Put behind thee ikon-worship.

Be faithful to thine over-lord,
Be true to thy King in every need,
Be true to thine own self besides,
True to thy High-King above all obstacles.

Do not malign any man,
Lest thou thyself maligned shouldst be,
And shouldst thou travel ocean and earth,
Follow the very steps of God's Anointed.

    CG

### Going to Church for the Sunday Eucharist

Euros Bowen, the Welsh priest and poet, remembers Gwilym,
Archbishop of Wales, presiding at the altar in the Bryn Mel chapel on
Anglesey:

*NID SIMBOLAU'N...*

The Reredos was not
an ecclesiastical adornment
of symbols,
but plain glass,
with the danger
of distracting the celebrant
from
the properties of the communion table,

for
in the translucence
the green earth
budded in the morning view,
the river was in bloom,
the air a joyous flight,
and the sunshine
set the clouds ablaze,

and I noticed
the priest's eyes
as it were unconsciously
placing his hand
on those gifts,
as though these
were
the bread and the wine.

*REREDOS*

(TR. EUROS BOWEN)

**The Lord of the Resurrection**

The Lord of the Resurrection is everywhere; in every living particle, every fireball, every unit of energy, every void.

I had the opportunity today to look at a vast view. Apart from the sea and the clouds and the sky there was none of nature's beauty in it; a large town with its industries and houses, and beyond it, the greyish sea, mist, cloud and the tender immensity of the sky; little men and their limited, raw busyness, and around them the stupefying abundance of the whole world; chattering, grunting, smiling sardonically and mouthing and around everything all the excellence of the limitless mercy.

And I felt that we were not worthy of the Christ who is in the creation. Every movement, every breathing, every crystallizing, every response to sun and shadow – is not the same power here as in the Resurrection?

*CUDD FY MEIAU*
PENNAR DAVIES
(TR. C. & S. DAVIES)

## PRAYER AT DRESSING

My mother would be asking us to sing our morning song to God down in the back-house, as Mary's lark was singing it up in the clouds, and as Christ's mavis[2] was singing it yonder in the tree, giving glory to the God of the creatures for the repose of the night, for the light of the day, and for the joy of life. She would tell us that every creature on the earth here below and in the ocean beneath and in the air above was giving glory to the great God of the creatures and the worlds, of the virtues and the blessings, and would *we* be dumb!

My dear mother reared her children in food and clothing, in love and charity. My heart loves the earth in which my beloved mother rests.

CG

&#9758;&#9759;

2.   mavis: song thrush.

# Midday

## SAIN FOR SHEEP

A prayer for protection and blessing made with the sign of the Cross.

The sain placed by Mary
    Upon her flock of sheep,
Against birds, against dogs,
    Against beasts, against men,
Against hounds, against thieves,
    Against polecats, against marten-cats,
Against eye, against envy,
    Against disease, against 'gaoban'.
In the hollow of your meeting,
    Be yours the aiding of God;
On the hillock of your lying,
    Whole be your rising.

*CG*

# A BLESSING FOR HEALTH AND HEALING CHARM

Living charm sent of quiet Brigit
    To Patrick noble, beauteous,
For wound, for worm,
For gulping throat,
    For rose, for swelling, for kidney,
For wounding, for festering,
For skin disease (?), for ulcer,
For serpent, for venom,
For illness in thy veins,
But be it for good and for excellence
    Upon thy flocks and upon thy herds;
If thou hast it up
Between the tips of thy two ears,
    Between the bases of thy two soles,
May it ebb from thee downward
As ebbs the ocean,
    Into the belly of the great whale
    And of beasts themselves,
    Till these divide each other;
As Jesus healed the people,
    It is in His nature to heal each of these distresses.
    CG

### Passing Thoughts

The world has laid low, and the wind blows away like ashes Alexander, Caesar, and all who were in their trust; Grass-grown is Tara, and see Troy now how it is – and the English themselves, perhaps they too will pass!

*IRISH SAYING* (17TH C. – 18TH C.)

AUTHOR UNKNOWN

(TR. K. H. JACKSON)

# Evening

BIRTH BAPTISM

When a child was born the midwife would put three small drops of water upon the forehead of the little one in name of Father, in name of Son, in name of Spirit, and she would say in this wise:

The little drop of the Father
    On thy little forehead, beloved one.

The little drop of the Son
    On thy little forehead, beloved one.

The little drop of the Spirit
    On thy little forehead, beloved one.

To aid thee from the fays,[3]
    To guard thee from the host;

To aid thee from the gnome,
    To shield thee from the spectre;

To keep thee for the Three,
    To shield thee, to surround thee;

To save thee for the Three,
    To fill thee with the graces;

The little drop of the Three
    To lave[4] thee with the graces.

Then the midwife would give the child to a nurse to wash it, and the
nurse would put a small palmful of water on the poor little infant, and
she would sing the sweetest music that ever ear heard on earth, and
she would say in this wise:

A wavelet for thy form,
A wavelet for thy voice,
    A wavelet for thy sweet speech;

A wavelet for thy luck,
A wavelet for thy good,
    A wavelet for thy health;

A wavelet for thy throat,
A wavelet for thy pluck,
    A wavelet for thy graciousness;
    Nine waves for thy graciousness.
    CG


3.    fays: doom of death.
4.    to lave: to lavish.

# PEACE

The peace of God, the peace of men,
The peace of Columba kindly,
The peace of Mary mild, the loving,
The peace of Christ, King of tenderness,
  The peace of Christ, King of tenderness.

Be upon each window, upon each door,
Upon each hole that lets in light,
Upon the four corners of my house,
Upon the four corners of my bed,
  Upon the four corners of my bed;

Upon each thing my eye takes in,
Upon each thing my mouth takes in,
Upon my body that is of earth
And upon my soul that came from on high,
  Upon my body that is of earth
  And upon my soul that came from on high.
  *CG*

### Meditation

Euros Bowen meditates on the need to keep the 'word of grace' firmly within its sacramental context, lest it be perverted into an 'ideology of Christ'.

### YN Y DIBRYDER BRYDERU...

In the anxiety which at the fair linen cloth
of our praise is free from care,
while for us there is the broken bread
and the peace from the word that speaks
of the wine given for an age set on the ideas
and practices of tomorrow's wrong,
let the blessed sustenance come from the heart of security
as confidence for men,
until it shall glow in the world
with the light which breaks forth from the mystery,
so that the word of grace shall not be an ideology of Christ.

*Y GAIR*

(TR. EUROS BOWEN)

# Nightfall

## SMOORING[5] THE FIRE

I smoor the fire this night
As the Son of Mary would smoor it;
The compassing of God be on the fire,
The compassing of God on all the household.

Be God's compassing about ourselves,
Be God's compassing about us all,
Be God's compassing upon the flock,
Be God's compassing upon the hearth.

Who keeps watch this night?
Who but the Christ of the poor,
The bright and gentle Brigit of the kine,[6]
The bright and gentle Mary of the ringlets.

Whole be house and herd,
Whole be son and daughter,
Whole be wife and man,
Whole be household all.

CG

5.    to smoor: to smother.
6.    kine: cattle.

### *Hymn*

According to Brendan O'Malley, Ann Griffiths (1776–1805) was 'arguably the greatest woman poet to have written in Welsh and undoubtedly a mystic in the great Celtic tradition.'

*DIOLCH BYTH, A CHANMIL DIOLCH...*

Thanks for ever,
and a hundred thousand thanks,
thanks while there is breath in me,
that there is an object to worship.

ANN GRIFFITHS

◎◎

# The Blessing

*BOED I FENDITH DUW SARA AC ABRAHAM...*

The blessing of the God of Sarah and of Abraham,
The blessing of the Son, born of Mary,
the blessing of the Holy Spirit who broods over us
    as a mother over her children,
be with you all.
Amen.

# 2 ◉ MONDAY

*Traditionally dedicated to the Holy Trinity,*
*three persons and one God.*

## Morning

PRAYER AT RISING

Thou King of moon and sun,
    Thou King of stars beloved,
Thou Thyself knowest our need,
    O Thou merciful God of life.

Each day that we move,
    Each time that we awaken,
Causing vexation and gloom
    To the King of hosts Who loved us.

Be with us through each day,
>Be with us through each night;
Be with us each night and day,
>Be with us each day and night.
>CG


## INVOCATION FOR JUSTICE

I will wash my face
In the nine rays of the sun,
As Mary washed her Son
>In the rich fermented milk.

Love be in my countenance,
Benevolence in my mind,
Dew of honey in my tongue,
>My breath as the incense.

Black is yonder town,
Black are those therein,
I am the white swan,
>Queen above them.

I will travel in the name of God,
In likeness of deer, in likeness of horse,
In likeness of serpent, in likeness of King;
>Stronger will it be with me than with all persons.
>CG

A LITTLE BOOK OF CELTIC PRAYER

***Thought for the Day***

*YR HOLL FYD SY'N LLAWN GOGONIANT:*

The whole world is full of glory.

Here is the glory of created things,
    the earth and the sky,
        the sun and the moon,
            the stars and the vast expanses:

Here is fellowship
    with all that was created,
        the air and the wind,
            cloud and rain,
                sunshine and snow:

All life like the bubbling of a flowing river
    and the dark currents of the depths of the sea
        is full of glory.

*GLORIA*

EUROS BOWEN

(TR. C. DAVIES)

*The Consecration of Daily Work*

## HERDING BLESSING

Travelling moorland, travelling townland,
Travelling mossland long and wide,
Be the herding of God the Son about your feet,
Safe and whole may ye home return,
    Be the herding of God the Son about your feet,
    Safe and whole may ye home return.

The sanctuary of Carmac and of Columba
Be protecting you going and coming,
And of the milkmaid of the soft palms,
Bride of the clustering hair golden brown,
    And of the milkmaid of the soft palms,
    Bride of the clustering hair golden brown.
    *CG*

# HUNTING BLESSING

A young man was consecrated before he went out to hunt. Oil was put on his head, a bow was placed in his hand, and he was required to stand with bare feet on the bare, grassless ground. The dedication of the young hunter was akin to those of the 'maor', the judge, the chief and the king, on installation. Many conditions were imposed on the young man, which he was required to observe throughout life.

From my loins begotten wert thou, my son,
May I guide thee the way that is right,
In the holy name of the apostles eleven
In name of the Son of God torn of thee.

In name of James, and Peter, and Paul,
John the baptist, and John the apostle above,
Luke the physician, and Stephen the martyr,
Muriel the fair, and Mary mother of the Lamb.

In name of Patrick holy of the deeds,
And Carmac of the rights and tombs,
Columba beloved, and Adamnan of laws,
Fite calm, and Bride of the milk and kine.

In name of Michael chief of hosts,
In name of Ariel youth of lovely hues,
In name of Uriel of the golden locks,
And Gabriel seer of the Virgin of grace.

The time thou shalt have closed thine eye,
Thou shalt not bend thy knee nor move,
Thou shalt not wound the duck that is swimming,
Never shalt thou harry her of her young.

The white swan of the sweet gurgle,
The speckled dun of the brown tuft,
Thou shalt not cut a feather from their backs,
Till the doom-day, on the crest of the wave.

On the wing be they always
Ere thou place missile to thine ear,
And the fair Mary will give thee of her love,
And the lovely Bride will give thee of her kine.

Thou shalt not eat fallen fish nor fallen flesh,
Nor one bird that thy hand shall not bring down,
Be thou thankful for the one,
Though nine should be swimming.

The fairy swan of Bride of flocks,
The fairy duck of Mary of peace.

CG

### Poem for the Day

Under the surface of Welsh religious poetry there is sometimes an impatience with the institutions of the Church, and of their conventional – and sometimes unreal – imagery.

## I BELIEVE

*... Pa beth a wnawn ...*

... What shall we do
with the pansy Christ
who hangs high
on the walls of the memory's vestries?

We shall tear
the petticoat that is about him
so that we see the eternal arms,
all hair and muscles,
and the hands like shovels
whipping synod and government.

Under the dirty marks
of the inquisitive fingers of the years
and the vestry and the Vatican's
layers of old varnish,
is the original portrait
of the Artisan from Nazareth

dismantling the grand furniture,
putting the rough crossbeam of his justice
and the long plank of his love
together,
binding them tightly
with the thong of his tough body.

I see this one today coming towards me
across *Tir Coch*,
beckoning with the hands
that are warm with his own blood.
I hear him call too
in the accents of *Nant Conwy*.

*CREDAF*

MERION EVANS

(TR. C. DAVIES)

## Thoughts, Pilgrims and Recollections

**When Christian Met Celt – Who Assimilated Whom?**

In my Irish Catholic boyhood we drank a curious soup of religion and mythology, rich and viscous but with a bitter-sweet taste, comforting yet warming. The ingredients – though never officially twinned – were the sober Christianity of Patrick and the wild paganism of the Celt.

So close the relationship, so alive the pagan history of this Isle of saints and scholars, that if a bunch of time-travelling, horse-borne Celtic warriors had turned up at Mass on a Sunday morning my eyes would have been surprised – but not my imagination, nor my faith.

They would have been welcomed, baptized, christened, and sent away as newly meek as that King at Cashel who suffered a crozier through his foot.

*THE CELTS*

F. DELANEY

◎◎

# Midday

## DRIVING THE COWS

The man or woman, youth or maiden, who goes 'a' saodach (sao-dachadh) a' chruidh', driving the cows, to the morning pastures, sings a song to the flock as they move leisurely along. The melody is very pleasing to man and evidently to beast. The song commends the cattle to the keeping of Mary the mild, to the keeping of Brigit the fair, and to the keeping of Michael the valiant, whose sword is sharp but whose shield is strong...

The person who goes to bring the cattle home probably meets them coming on their way. When they come in sight, the man or woman, youth or maiden, addresses them in a rich variety of endearing terms, and as he draws nearer he strikes up a song of welcome to the cattle, 'fàilte a' chruidh', to which they respond with a low modulated moan, sometimes breaking forth into a bellow. Some cow has hustled her way to the front, and the rest follow her as a leader. The bull always brings up the rear.

CG

Closed to you be every pit,
Smooth to you be every hill,
Snug to you be every bare spot,
        Beside the cold mountains.

The sanctuary of Mary Mother be yours,
The sanctuary of Brigit the loved be yours,
The sanctuary of Michael victorious be yours,
        Active and full be you gathered home.

The protection of shapely Cormac be yours,
The protection of Brendan of the ship be yours,
The protection of Maol Duinne the saint be yours
        In marshy ground and rocky ground.

The fellowship of Mary Mother be yours,
The fellowship of Brigit of kine be yours,
The fellowship of Michael victorious be yours,
        In nibbling, in chewing, in munching.
        CG

# CHARM FOR THE EVIL EYE

An eye was seeing thee,
    A mouth had named thee,
A heart has thought of thee,
    A mind has desired thee.

May Three Persons sanctify thee,
    May Three Persons aid thee,
The Father and the Son
    And the perfect Spirit.

Four have wrought thy hurt,
    A man and a woman,
        A lad and a maiden;

Three I set to oppose them,
    Father and Son
        And Holy Spirit.

Who is it that repels them?
    Who is it that averts them?
The Three Persons of the Blessed Trinity,
    The Three Persons of the Triune.
    CG

## *Wishes, Tales and Longings*

### The Island Hermitage of Colmcille

An unknown Irish writer meditates upon Colmcille's (Columba's) retreat on the Isle of Iona some six centuries before.

Delightful I think it is to be in the bosom of an isle, on the peak of a rock, that I might often see there the calm of the sea.

That I might see its heavy waves over the glittering ocean, as they chant a melody to the Father on their eternal course.

That I might see its smooth strand of clear headlands, no gloomy thing; that I might hear the voice of the wondrous birds, a joyful tune.

That I might hear the sound of the shallow waves against the rocks; that I might hear the cry by the graveyard, the noise of the sea.

That I might see its splendid flocks of birds over the full-watered ocean; that I might see its mighty waves, greatest of wonders.

That I might see its ebb and its flood tide in their flow; that this might be my name, a secret I tell, 'He who turned his back on Ireland'.

That contrition of heart should come upon me as I watch it; that I might bewail my many sins, difficult to declare.

That I might bless the Lord who has power over all, Heaven with its pure host of angels, earth, ebb, floodtide.

That I might pore on one of my books, good for my soul; a while kneeling for beloved Heaven, a while at psalms.

A while gathering dulse[1] from the rock, a while fishing, a while giving food to the poor, a while in my cell.

A while meditating upon the Kingdom of Heaven, holy is the redemption; a while at labour not too heavy; it would be delightful!

IRISH (12TH C.)
AUTHOR UNKNOWN
(TR. K. H. JACKSON)

### Passing Thoughts
*Is miath am buachaill an oidhche: bheir i dhachaidh gach beathach is duine.*

Night is a good shepherd: it brings home every man and beast.

☉☉

---

1. dulse: seaweed.

# Evening

## THE SUN

Old men in the Isles still uncover their heads when they first see the sun on coming out in the morning.

The eye of the great God,
The eye of the God of glory,
The eye of the King of hosts,
The eye of the King of the living,
    Pouring upon us
        At each time and season,
    Pouring upon us
        Gently and generously.

        Glory to thee,
            Thou glorious sun.

        Glory to thee, thou sun,
            Face of the God of life.

CG

# THE BAPTISM BY THE KNEE-WOMAN

When the child comes into the world, the knee-woman puts three drops of water on the forehead of the poor little infant, who has come home to us from the bosom of the everlasting Father. And the woman does this in the name and in the reverence of the kind and powerful Trinity, and says thus:

In name of God,
In name of Jesus,
In name of Spirit,
The perfect Three of power.

The little drop of the Father
On thy little forehead, beloved one.

The little drop of the Son
On thy little forehead, beloved one.

The little drop of the Spirit
On thy little forehead, beloved one.

To aid thee, to guard thee,
To shield thee, to surround thee.

To keep thee from the fays,
To shield thee from the host.

To sain thee from the gnome,
To deliver thee from the spectre.

The little drop of the Three
To shield thee from the sorrow.

The little drop of the Three
To fill thee with Their pleasantness.

The little drop of the Three
To fill thee with Their virtue.

O the little drop of the Three
To fill thee with Their virtue.

CG

☺☺

# Nightfall

## THE HOMESTEAD

O God, bless my homestead,
    Bless Thou all therein.

O God, bless my kindred,
    Bless Thou my substance.

O God, bless my words,
    Bless Thou my converse.

O God, bless my errand,
    Bless Thou my journey.

O God, lessen my sin,
    Increase Thou my trust.

O God, ward from me distress.
    Ward Thou from me misfortune.

O God, shield me from guilt,
    Fill Thou me with joy.

And, O God, let naught to my body
That shall do harm to my soul

When I enter the fellowship
    Of the great Son of Mary.
      CG

**Hymn**

*O  AM  BARA  I  UCHEL  YFED...*

Let me drink for ever deeply
of salvation's mighty flood,
till I thirst no more for ever
after any earthly good.
    ANN GRIFFITHS

◉◉

# The Blessing

May the eye of the great God
The eye of the God of glory,
The eye of the Virgin's Son,
The eye of the gentle Spirit
  Aid you and shepherd you
    In every time,
  Pour upon you every hour
    Mildly and generously.

CG

# 3 ◉ TUESDAY

*Traditionally dedicated to St Michael and the holy angels.*

## Morning

### PRAYER AT DRESSING

My mother was always at work, by day helping my father on the croft, and by night at wool and at spinning, at night clothes and at day clothes for the family. My mother would be beseeching us to be careful in everything, to put value on time and eschew idleness; that a night was coming in which no work could be done. She would be telling us about Mac Shiamain,[1] and how he sought to be at work. If we were dilatory in putting on our clothes, and made an excuse for our prayers, my mother would say that God regarded heart and not speech, the mind and not the manner; and that we might clothe our souls with grace while clothing our bodies with raiment. My mother taught us what we should ask for in the prayer, as she had heard it from her own mother, and as she again heard it from the one who was before her.

Bless to me, O God,
My soul and body;
Bless to me, O God,
My belief and my condition;

Bless to me, O God,
My heart and my speech,
And bless to me, O God,
The handling of my hand;

Strength and busyness of morning,
Habit and temper of modesty,
Force and wisdom of thought,
And Thine own path, O God of virtues,
Till I go to sleep this night;

Thine own path, O God of virtues,
Till I go to sleep this night.

CG

1. Mac Shiamain: lit. son of straw-rope, i.e. the good husbandman.

DESIRES

May I speak this day according to Thy justice,
Each day may I show Thy chastening, O God;
May I speak each day according to Thy wisdom,
Each day and night may I be at peace with Thee.

Each day may I count the causes of Thy mercy,
May I each day give heed to Thy laws;
Each day may I compose to Thee a song,
May I harp each day Thy praise, O God.

May I each day give love to Thee, Jesu,
Each night may I do the same;
Each day and night, dark and light,
May I laud Thy goodness to me, O God.

CG

## *Thought for the Day*

*Tybir yn aml mai lluosogrwydd ei threfydd mawrion yw cyfoeth gwlad, lle
mae peiriannau yn fwy pwysig nag eneidiau; ond gwir olud gwlad yw'r
lleoedd bychan a fu'n gartref ei dysgawdwyr ac yn fagwrle ei meddwl.*

It is often thought that the riches of a country are its multiplicity of
large towns, where machines are more important than souls; but the
little places that were the homes of its educators and the nurseries of
its mind are the wealth of a country.

O. M. EDWARDS
(TR. C. DAVIES)

## The Consecration of Daily Work

REAPING BLESSING

On Tuesday of the feast at the rise of the sun,
And the back of the ear of corn to the east,
I will go forth with my sickle under my arm,
And I will reap the cut the first act.

I will let my sickle down
While the fruitful ear is in my grasp,
I will raise mine eye upwards,
I will turn me on my heel quickly,

Rightway as travels the sun
From the airt[2] of the east to the west,
From the airt of the north with motion calm
To the very core of the airt of the south.

I will give thanks to the King of grace
For the growing crops of the ground,
He will give food to ourselves and to the flocks
According as He disposeth to us.

James and John, Peter and Paul,
Mary beloved, the fullness of light.

On Michaelmas Eve and Christmas,
We will all taste of the bannock.[3]

CG

### *Poem for the Day*

In this poem (the only one in this collection that was written in
English), as well as in the prose passage that follows it, there occurs
the untranslatable Welsh word 'hiraeth' which may be likened to a
nameless woe, a deep spirit of longing.

## A CELTIC CHRIST

The Celtic fabric of Christ's mystery
Was woven in the knotwork of old dreams,
A warp of myth, a weft of history
Loomed beside silver, salmon-knowing streams.

Destiny's fibre teased in star-spun strands
Woven upon Arianrhod's silver wheel,
Woven for virgin Brigid's milk-white hands
Set on the shoulders of the myth made real.

---

2.  airt: the quarter of the heavens; the point of the compass; the direction of the wind.
3.  bannock: oatcake.

The sevenfold sun God's sandals touch the land,
The Druid's hope is more than hope – fulfilled,
The bread of being breaks between his hands,
His salt sharp blood is voluntarily spilled.

A Lleu Llaw[4] greater than the bards had dreamed
Comes to receive the lance's thrust in time,
Once upon a time in real time redeemed,
The word made flesh from every bardic rhyme.

Dance with the ancient gods while yet you may
From every blood-grim grove set free the fear,
Your golden time ebbs with this Celtic day
As Petrine Rome hefts yet another spear.

They sought in synods to suppress your smile,
They sealed your cairn up with expediency,
They put your words on theologic trial,
Their holy keys set power's prim zealots free.

Yet like the eagle soul of murdered Lleu
You bide your time upon your holy tree.
Then as I make my hiraeth's sacred vow
You answer and descend to stand with me.

M. T. HARRIS

4. Lleu Llaw: from the collection of Welsh medieval romances known as the
   *Mabinogion*; a young prince who is betrayed and murdered with a poisoned lance,
   and then lovingly restored to life and victory; fulfilled in Christ.

## Thoughts, Pilgrimages and Recollections

### A Welsh Pilgrimage

All pilgrims might be defined as persons who undertake journeys for a religious purpose, a quest with a hidden spiritual meaning. There is a sublime analogy between such definite journeys and an individual's journey through life. Personal transformation always takes place in the pilgrimage …

The pilgrimage is the emblem of our life, the symbol of our being; but life isn't hurrying on, it is standing aside to witness the eternity within. With every step we take on our journey to a holy place, hallowed by the sacred journeys of those who have gone before, there is the equal quest for the place where God rests, at the very centre of our heart …

It is therefore possible to experience through the act of pilgrimage a sacramental encounter with the Incarnate God, present both within the traveller and the planet through which he walks.

It is a question of spiritual integration with the Creator God. The desire to see, find and experience the Risen Christ both within and without produces a thirst and a longing to see the Face of God. It may be likened to a nameless woe, or hiraeth, that untranslatable Welsh word which constitutes a deep spirit of longing …

'Walking Prayer' has a goal, both physical and mental, in God. In our mind's eye we journey towards someone we love and this constant state of expectancy raises our spirits and lessens our mental stress or fatigue. We walk towards the Divine Lover and constantly repeat 'Lord Jesus Christ, Son of God, have mercy on me a sinner' and combine the sentence with our breath in rhythm with the movements of our body.

With this prayer and the forward impulsion of our body we are taken up, as it were, into the care of our heavenly Father.

INTRODUCTION TO *CYDYMAITH Y PERERIN*

B. O'MALLEY

# Midday

## CHARM OF THE BUTTER

The charm made of Columba
To the maiden of the glen,
Her butter to make more,
Her milk to make surpassing.

Come, ye rich lumps, come!
Come, ye rich lumps, come!
Come, ye rich lumps, masses large,
Come, ye rich lumps, come!

Thou Who put beam in moon and sun,
Thou Who put food in ear and herd,
Thou Who put fish in stream and sea,
Send the butter up betimes!

Come, ye rich lumps, come!
Come, ye rich lumps, come!
Come, ye rich lumps, masses large,
Come, ye rich lumps, come!

CG

# KIDNEY OF MARY[5]

Kidney of Mary, 'tearna Moire', saving of Mary. This is a square, thick Atlantic nut, sometimes found indented along and across, the indentations forming a natural cross on the nut. It is occasionally mounted in silver and hung around the neck as a talisman. Every nurse[6] has one which she places in the hand of the woman to increase her faith and distract her attention. It was consecrated on the altar and much venerated.

'Behold, O Mary Mother,
    The woman and she near to death.'
'Behold Thou her, O Christ,
    Since it is of Thy mercy
To give rest to the child
    And to bring this woman from her labour.

'Behold Thou her, O Christ,
    Since Thou art the King of health,
Deliver the woman from death
    And sain the innocent child,
Give Thou rest to the vine-shoot,
    Give Thou peace to its mother.'
    CG

5.    Kidney of Mary: a charm for a difficult labour.
6.    nurse: village midwife in the Western Isles in the nineteenth century.

## *Wishes, Tales and Longings*

In the eighth and ninth centuries, there was a tendency among solitary contemplatives in Ireland and Scotland to band together in groups of 13 (suggestive of Christ and his 12 apostles). These were known as the *Culdees* (from the Irish *cele de*, meaning 'companions').

The following tenth-century fragment illustrates the longing of one unknown Irishman to enter upon the *Culdee* way of life.

### The Wish of Manchan Of Laith

I wish, O son of the Living God, ancient eternal Kind, for a secret hut in the wilderness, that it may be my dwelling.

A very blue shallow well to be beside it, a clear pool for washing away sins through the grace of the Holy Ghost.

A beautiful wood close by around it on every side, for the nurture of many voiced birds, to shelter and hide it.

Facing the south for warmth, a little stream across its enclosure, a choice ground with abundant bounties which would be good for every plant.

A few sage disciples, I will tell their number, humble and obedient, to pray to the King.

Four threes, three fours, fit for every need, two sixes in the church, both south and north.

Six couples in addition to me myself, praying through the long ages to the King who moves the sun.

A lovely church decked with linen, a dwelling for God of Heaven; then, bright candles over the holy white Scriptures.

One room to go to for the care of the body, without wantonness, without voluptuousness, without meditation of evil.

This is the housekeeping I would undertake, I would choose it without concealing; fragrant fresh leeks, hens, speckled salmon, bees.

My fill of clothing and of food from the King of good fame, and for me to be sitting for a while praying to God in every place.

*IRISH* (10TH C.)
AUTHOR UNKNOWN
(TR. K. H. JACKSON)

## *Passing Thoughts*

### A Vain Pilgrimage

Coming to Rome, much labour and little profit! The King whom you seek here, unless you bring Him with you you will not find Him!

*IRISH SAYING* (9TH C.)
AUTHOR UNKNOWN
(TR. K. H. JACKSON)

☺☺

# Evening

## DEATH

The tune was played at funerals in Lewis, Harris and Skye down to Disruption times. I spoke to people who had heard it played at a funeral at Aoidh, in Lewis. They said that the scene and the tune were singularly impressive – the moaning of the sea, the mourning of the women, and the lament of the pipes over all as the body was carried to its home of winter, to its home of autumn, of spring and of summer; never could they forget the solemnity of the occasion, where all was so natural and so beautiful, and nature seemed to join in the feelings of humanity.

I am going home with thee
    To thy home! to thy home!
I am going home with thee
    To thy home of winter.

I am going home with thee
    To thy home! to thy home!
I am going home with thee
    To thy home of autumn, of spring and of summer.

I am going home with thee,
    Thou child of my love,
To thine eternal bed,
    To thy perpetual sleep.

I am going home with thee,
    Thou child of my love,
To the dear Son of blessings,
    To the Father of grace.
    CG


## THE MOTHER'S PARTING BLESSING

When a son or a daughter is leaving home in the Western Isles, the event is warmly felt, for the feelings of the people are deep and strong, if silent and subdued. Friends and neighbours come to say farewell to the pilgrim, and to pray for peace and prosperity in the adopted land. Before crossing the threshold of the old home, a parting hymn is sung … These parting scenes are less common now than they were in the past.

The benison[7] of God be to thee,
The benison of Christ be to thee,
The benison of Spirit be to thee,
And to thy children,
    To thee and to thy children.

The peace of God be to thee,
The peace of Christ be to thee,
The peace of Spirit be to thee,
During all thy life,
    All the days of thy life.

The keeping of God upon thee in every pass,
The shielding of Christ upon thee in every path,
The bathing of Spirit upon thee in every stream,
    In every land and sea thou goest.

The keeping of the everlasting Father be thine
    Upon His own illumined altar;
The keeping of the everlasting Father be thine
    Upon his own illumined altar.
    *CG*

7.    benison: blessing.

# Nightfall

## ENCOMPASSING OF FAMILY

Bless, O God, the fire,
    As Thou didst bless the Virgin;
Bless, O God, the hearth,
As Thou didst bless the Sabbath.

Bless, O God, the household,
    According as Jesus said;
Bless, O God, the family,
    As becomes us to offer it.

Bless, O God, the house,
    Bless, O God, the fire,
Bless, O God, the hearth;
    Be Thyself our stay.

        May the Being of life bless,
        May the Christ of love bless,
        May the Spirit Holy bless
    Each one and all,
    Every one and all.
    CG

### *Hymn*

*EI LAW ASWY SY'N FY NGHYNNAL...*

His left hand, in heat of noon day,
lovingly my head upholds,
and his right hand, filled with blessings
tenderly my soul enfolds.

ANN GRIFFITHS

# The Blessing

God's grace distil on you,
Christ's grace distil on you,
Spirit's grace distil on you
    Each day and each night
        Of your portion in the world;
    On each day and each night
        Of your portion in the world.

CG

# 4 ✆ WEDNESDAY

*Traditionally dedicated to the holy Apostles.*

## Morning

THANKSGIVING

Thanks to Thee, O God, that I have risen today,
　　To the rising of this life itself;
May it be to Thine own glory, O God of every gift,
　　And to the glory of my soul likewise.

O great God, aid Thou my soul
　　With the aiding of Thine own mercy;
Even as I clothe my body with wool,
　　Cover Thou my soul with the shadow of Thy wing.

Help me to avoid every sin,
    And the source of every sin to forsake;
And as the mist scatters on the crest of the hills,
    May each ill haze clear from my soul, O God.
    CG


## COME I THIS DAY

Come I this day to the Father,
Come I this day to the Son,
Come I to the Holy Spirit powerful;
Come I this day with God,
Come I this day with Christ,
Come I with the Spirit of kindly balm.

God, and Spirit, and Jesus,
From the crown of my head
To the soles of my feet;
Come I with my reputation,
Come I with my testimony,
Come I to Thee, Jesu –
    Jesu, shelter me.
    CG


***Thought for the Day***
*Gwarchod i mi fy nhraed ar dir tirion Cymru.*

Guard for me my feet upon the gentle earth of Wales.

## *The Consecration of Daily Work*

## LOOM BLESSING

Thrums[1] nor odds of thread
My hand never kept, nor shall keep,

Every colour in the bow of the shower
Has gone through my fingers beneath the cross,

White and black, red and madder,[2]
Green, dark grey, and scarlet,

Blue, and roan and colour of the sheep,
And never a particle of cloth was wanting.

I beseech calm Bride the generous,
I beseech mild Mary the loving,
I beseech Christ Jesu the humane,
That I may not die without them,

>   That I may not die without them.

>   CG

---

1.    thrum: thread.

2.    madder: dye gathered from a herbaceous climbing plant with yellowish flowers.

# THE BLESSING OF THE PARCHING

When it is necessary to provide a small quantity of meal hastily, ears of corn are plucked and placed in a net made of the tough roots of the yellow bedstraw, bent, or quicken grass, and hung above a slow smokeless fire. The bag is taken down now and again to turn the ears of corn. This net, however, can only be used for bere or barley; rye and oats, being more detachable, require the use of a pot or 'tarran' to dry them. This mode of drying corn is called 'fuirireadh', parching, and the corn 'fuirireach', parched. The meal ground from the grain is called 'min fhuiriridh', parched meal. Bread made of meal thus prepared has a strong peaty flavour much relished by the people.

Thou flame grey, slender, curved,
Coming from the top pore of the peat,
Thou flame of leaps, breadth, heat,
Come not nigh me with thy quips.

A burning steady, gentle, generous,
Coming round about my quicken roots,
A fire fragrant, fair, and peaceful,
Nor causes dust, nor grief, nor havoc.

Heat, parch my fat seed,
For food for my little child,
In name of Christ, King of the elements,
Who gave us corn and bread and blessing withal,
    In name of Christ, King of the elements,
    Who gave us corn and bread and blessing withal.
    CG

## *Poem for the Day*

## THE CHRIST OF NATURE

He loved cherry sunsets growing heavy on the branches of the
    evening;
He loved bud coloured dawns opening from the east's earth.

He loved the sea, green in its happiness, seeking the shore;
He loved to see it languishing back stonily from its crest to its groove.

He loved the character of birds, the flock that trusted in His Father;
He loved lambs, the most skilfully fashioned; the lambs, the most
    innocent their nature.

He loved the beasts of the borders: the ones that dwelt in the wild;
He loved their sure dependence on that which the wilderness
    provided.

He loved wheat shivering as it became golden and heavy headed with
    nourishment;
He loved the fortressed mountain country, the desolation where
    peace grew.

He loved the earth, loved it as a lover, because it is God's earth;
He loved it, because it was created by His Father from nothingness to
    be Life's temple.

*CRIST NATUR*
DONALD EVANS
(TR. C. DAVIES)

◎◎

# Midday

## PRAYER OF THE TEATS

Teat of Mary,
Teat of Brigit,
Teat of Michael,
    Teat of God.

No malice shall lie,
No envy shall lie,
No eye shall lie
    Upon my heart's dear one.

No fear shall lie,
No ill-will shall lie,
No loss shall lie
    On my own 'Mìneag'.[3]

No spell shall lie,
No spite shall lie
On her beneath the keeping
    Of the King of the stars;
On her beneath the keeping
    Of the King of the stars.

3.    mìneag: gentle.

In sitting down to milk the cow the woman says or sings or intones a short rhythmical prayer.

Bless, O God, my little cow,
    Bless, O God, my desire;
Bless Thou my partnership
    And the milking of my hands, O God.

Bless, O God, each teat,
    Bless, O God, each finger;
Bless Thou each drop
    That goes into my pitcher, O God!

After this prayer the woman sings songs and croons, lilts and lullabies, to cow after cow till all are milked.

    CG

## CHARM FOR CHEST SEIZURE

The 'chest seizure' was much dreaded throughout the Highlands and Islands. In the old *Statistical Account of Scotland* the Rev. Dr Thomas Bisset of Logierait says: 'There is a disease called "glacach" by the Highlanders, which, as it affects the chest and lungs, is evidently of a consumptive nature.'

I will heal thee,
    Mary will heal with me,
Mary and Michael and Brigit
    Be with me all three.

Thy strait and thy sickness
    Be upon the earth holes,
Be on the grey stones,
    Since they have firmest base.

Be upon the birds of the sky,
    Be upon the wasps of the knolls,
Be upon the whales of the sea,
    Since they have swiftest body.

Be upon the clouds of the skies,
    Since they are pronest to rain,
Be upon the stream of the river
    Whirling to the wave.

### *Wishes, Tales and Longings*

A love of nature and a compassion for all creatures is a central feature of both Celtic literature and Celtic spirituality. There is very little of that false dichotomy of 'sacred' and 'secular' which is such a feature of mainstream Western culture for, to the Celt, the whole of life and the whole of creation is sacred.

### Suibhne, the Wild Man in the Forest

Little antlered one, little belling one, melodious little bleater, sweet I think the lowing that you make in the glen.

Homesickness for my little dwelling has come upon my mind, the calves in the plain, the deer on the moor.

Oak, bushy, leafy, you are high above trees; hazel bush, little branchy one, coffer of hazelnuts.

Alder, you are not spiteful, lovely is your colour, you are not prickly where you are in the gap.

Blackthorn, little thorny one, black little sloe bush; watercress, little green-topped one, on the brink of the blackbird's well.

Saxifrage of the pathway, you are the sweetest of herbs; cress, very green one; plant where the strawberry grows.

Apple tree, little apple tree, violently everyone shakes you; rowan, little berried one, lovely is your bloom.

Bramble, little humped one, you do not grant fair terms; you do not cease tearing me till you are sated with blood.

Yew, little yew, you are conspicuous in graveyards; ivy, little ivy, you are familiar in the dark wood.

Holly, little shelterer, door against the wind; ash tree, baneful, weapon in the hand of a warrior.

Birch, smooth, blessed, proud, melodious, lovely is each entangled branch at the top of your crest.

Aspen as it trembles, from time to time I hear its leaves rustling, and think it is the foray ...

If on my lonely journey I were to search the mountains of the dark earth, I would rather have the room for a single hut in great Glenn mBolcáin.

Good is its clear blue water, good its clean stern wind, good its cress-green watercress, better its deep brooklime.

Good its pure ivy, good its bright merry willow, good its yewy yew, better its melodious birch ...

*IRISH VERSE* (12TH C.)
AUTHOR UNKNOWN
(TR. K. H. JACKSON)

### Passing Thoughts

*Cha n-eil mi 'nam sgoilear 's cha n-àill leam a bhi – mar a thubhairt am madadh ruadh ris a' mhadadh.*

I am no scholar and I don't want to be one – as the fox said to the wolf.

✹

# Evening

## THE NEW MOON

When a person sees the new moon, he ought to make a reverence to it, and to make the cross of Christ over the tablet of his heart, and to say the rune in the eye of the God of glory Who sees all.

May thy light be fair to me!
May thy course be smooth to me!
If good to me is thy beginning,
Seven times better be thine end,
    Thou fair moon of the seasons,
    Thou great lamp of grace!

He Who created thee
    Created me likewise;
He Who gave thee weight and light
    Gave to me life and death,
    And the joy of the seven satisfactions,
    Thou great lamp of grace,
    Thou fair moon of the seasons.
    CG

# PETITION

Be Thou a smooth way before me,
Be Thou a guiding star above me,
Be Thou a keen eye behind me,
This day, this night, for ever.

I am weary, and I forlorn,
Lead Thou me to the land of the angels;
Methinks it were time I went for a space
To the court of Christ, to the peace of heaven;

If only Thou, O God of life,
Be at peace with me, be my support,
Be to me as a star, be to me as a helm,
From my lying down in peace to my rising anew.

CG

☺☺

# Nightfall

## SLEEP INVOCATION

I lie down this night
    With Brigit of the mantles,
With Mary of peace,
    With Jesus of the poor.

I lie down this night
    With Brigit of calmness,
With Mary revered,
    With Michael of my love.

I lie down this night
    Near the King of life,
Near Christ of the destitute,
    Near the Holy Spirit.

I lie down this night
    With the nine crosses holy,
From the crown of my head
    To the soles of my feet;
        From the crown of my head
           To the soles of my feet.

CG

## *Hymn*

*MYFI A ANTURIAF YNO YN EON...*

Boldly will I venture forward;
see the golden sceptre shine;
pointing straight towards the sinner,
all may enter by that sign.

ANN GRIFFITHS

◎◎

# The Blessing

God's blessing be yours,
    And well may it befall you;
Christ's blessing be yours,
    And well be you entreated;
Spirit's blessing be yours,
    And well spend you your lives,
        Each day that you rise up,
            Each night that you lie down.

*CG*

# 5 ⊛ THURSDAY

*Traditionally dedicated to the Holy Spirit;*
*also in thanksgiving for the Holy Eucharist.*

## Morning

PRAYER AT RISING

Bless to me, O God,
    Each thing mine eye sees;
Bless to me, O God,
    Each sound mine ear hears;
Bless to me, O God,
    Each odour that goes to my nostrils;
Bless to me, O God,
    Each taste that goes to my lips;
    Each note that goes to my song,
    Each ray that guides my way,
    Each thing that I pursue,

Each lure that tempts my will,
   The zeal that seeks my living soul,
The Three that seek my heart,
   The zeal that seeks my living soul,
The Three that seek my heart.

CG

## PRAYER FOR VICTORY

I bathe my face
In the nine rays of the sun,
As Mary bathed her Son
   In the rich fermented milk.

Honey be in my mouth,
Affection be in my face;
The love that Mary gave her Son
   Be in the heart of all flesh for me.

All-seeing, all-hearing, all-inspiring may God be,
To satisfy and to strengthen me;
Blind, deaf, and dumb, ever, ever be
   My contemners and my mockers,

The tongue of Columba in my head,
The eloquence of Columba in my speech;
The composure of the Victorious Son of grace
Be mine in presence of the multitude.

CG

### Thought for the Day

*Tigh gun chù gun chat gun leanabh beag, tigh gun ghean gun ghàire.*

A house without a dog, a cat, or a little child is one without affection
or merriment.

### The Consecration of Daily Work

## THE CHANT OF THE WARPING

Thursday of beneficence,
For warping and waulking,[1]
An hundred and fifty strands there shall be
To number.

Blue thread, very fine,
Two of white by its side,
And scarlet by the side
Of the madder.

1. waulking: the fulling of cloth.

My warp shall be very even,
Give to me Thy blessing, O God,
And to all who are beneath my roof
    In the dwelling.

Michael, thou angel of power,
Mary fair, who art above,
Christ, Thou Shepherd of the people,
Do ye your eternal blessing
    Bestow

On each one who shall lie down,
In the name of the Father and of Christ,
And of the Spirit of peacefulness,
    And of grace.

Sprinkle down on us like dew
The gracious wisdom of the mild woman,
Who neglected never the guidance
    Of the High King.

Ward away every evil eye,
And all people of evil wishes,
Consecrate the woof and the warp
    Of every thread.

Place Thou Thine arm around
Each woman who shall be waulking it,
And do Thou aid her in the hour
> Of her need.

Give to me virtues abundant
As Mary had in her day,
That I may possess the glory
> Of the High King.

Since Thou, O God, it is who givest growth,
To each species and kind,
Give us wool from the surface
> Of the green grass.

Consecrate the flock in every place,
With their little lambs melodious, innocent,
And increase the generations
> Of our herds.

So that we may obtain from them wool,
And nourishing milk to drink,
And that no dearth may be ours
> Of day clothing.
>> CG

# CLIPPING BLESSING

When a man has shorn a sheep and has set it free, he waves his hand
after it and says:

Go shorn and come woolly,
Bear the Beltane female lamb,
Be the lovely Bride thee endowing,
And the fair Mary thee sustaining,
    The fair Mary sustaining thee.

Michael the chief be shielding thee
From the evil dog and from the fox,
From the wolf and from the sly bear,
And from the taloned birds of destructive bills,
    From the taloned birds of hooked bills.

CG

*Poem for the Day*

## CROWS

Crows flying to their retreat in the wood's choir,
turning away beyond the road's rushing,
old ever-with-us things
like green, yellowish grey sins,
the generations of the leaves and oak trees' decay,
ministers under the raucous belfry of the parish,
in their black despite the broken altars of the druids,
at it now between the surpliced walls of heaven .
chanting the psalms of the day's meditations –
having long been shepherding the salt of the earth
in the light of the world on slope and on field,
listening to the treasure's seed
and pecking to the very heart
of the hidden wisdom between the rocks and the stones, –
and returning from the ravines' fragrances
to chancel and altar at nightfall
past the ebb and the flow, the ashes and the dust
with the mustard seeds of the pearl in their beak, –
the stewards of the blessed mysteries
under the hill's bells in the branched glory of the tree.

*BRAIN*

EUROS BOWEN

(TR. C. DAVIES)

# Midday

## COLUMBA'S HERDING

May the herding of Columba
Encompass you going and returning,
Encompass you in strath² and on ridge
    And on the edge of each rough region;

May it keep you from pit and from mire,
Keep you from hill and from crag,
Keep you from loch and from downfall,
    Each evening and each darkling;

May it keep you from the mean destroyer,
Keep you from the mischievous niggard,
Keep you from the mishap of bar-stumbing
    And from the untoward fays.

The peace of Columba be yours in the grazing,
The peace of Brigit be yours in the grazing,
The peace of Mary be yours in the grazing,
    And may you return home safe-guarded.
    CG

2.    strath: a broad, shallow valley.

# CHARM FOR CONSUMPTION

I trample on thee, evil wasting,
    As tramples swan on brine,
Thou wasting of back, thou wasting of body,
    Thou foul wasting of chest.

May Christ's own Gospel
    Be to make thee whole,
The Gospel of the Healer of healers,
    The Gospel of the God of grace,

To remove from thee thy sickness
    In the pool of health
From the crown of thy head
    To the base of thy two heels,

From thy two loins thither
    To thy two loins hither,
In reliance on the might of the God of Love
    And of the whole Powers together, –
        The love of grace!

CG

### Wishes, Tales and Longings

A religious poet imagines himself as a tributary tenant of God, rendering the Irish legal dues of lodging and entertainment to his overlord and his retinue.

K. H. JACKSON

## THE GREAT ALE-FEAST

I should like to have a great ale-feast for the King of Kings;
I should like the Heavenly Host to be drinking it for all eternity.

I should like to have the fruits of Faith, of pure devotion;
I should like to have the seats of Repentance in my house.

I should like to have the men of Heaven in my own dwelling;
I should like the tubs of Long-Suffering to be at their service.

I should like to have the vessels of Charity to dispense;
I should like to have the pitchers of Mercy for their company.

I should like there to be Hospitality for their sake;
I should like Jesus to be here always.

I should like to have the Three Marys of glorious renown;
I should like to have the Heavenly Host from every side.

I should like to be rent-payer to the Lord;
he to whom He gives a good blessing has done well in suffering
    distress.

*IRISH* (10TH C. – 11TH C.)

AUTHOR UNKNOWN

(TR. K. H. JACKSON)

### Passing Thoughts
*Cha leasachadh air droch obair latha a bhi fada gun tòiseachadh.*

Beginning late does not improve a bad day's work.


## A PRAYER FOR INTEGRITY

Be thou my vision, beloved Lord:
no other is aught but the King of the seven heavens.

Be thou my meditation by day and night:
may it be thou that I behold for ever in my sleep.

Be thou my speech, be thou my understanding:
be thou for me; may I be for thee.

Be thou my father; may I be thy son:
mayest thou be mine; may I be thine.

Be thou my battle-shield, be thou my sword:
be thou my honour, be thou my delight.

Be thou my shelter, be thou my stronghold:
mayest thou raise me up in the company of angels.

Be thou every good to my body and soul:
be thou my kingdom in heaven and earth.

Be thou alone my heart's special love:
let there be none other save the High-king of heaven.

To the King of all may I come after prized practice of devotion:
may I be in the kingdom of heaven in the brightness of the sun.

Beloved Father, hear my lamentation:
this miserable wretch (alas!) thinks it time.

Beloved Christ, whate'er befalls me:
O Ruler of all, be thou my vision.

> *IRISH* (8TH C.)
>
> (TR. MARY BYRNE)

☉☉

# Evening

## THE VIRGIN

The Virgin was beheld approaching,
Christ so young on her breast,
Angels bowing lowly before them,
And the King of life was saying, 'Tis meet.

The Virgin of locks most glorious,
The Jesus more gleaming-white than snow,
Seraphs melodious singing their praise,
And the King of life was saying, 'Tis meet.

O Mary Mother of wondrous power,
Grant us the succour of thy strength,
Bless the provision, bless the board,
Bless the ear, the corn, the food.

The Virgin of mien[3] most glorious,
The Jesus more gleaming-white than snow,
She like the moon on hills arising,
He like the sun on the mountain-crests.

> CG

3.   mien: bearing, displaying a person's character.

# A PRAYER FOR A JOYOUS DEATH

Give us, O God, the needs of the body,
    Give us, O God, the needs of the soul;
Give us, O God, the healing balsam of the body,
    Give us, O God, the healing balsam of the soul.

Give us, O God, the joy of repentance,
Give us, O God, the joy of forgiveness,
    Wash Thou from us the lees of corruption,
Cleanse Thou from us the stain of uncleanness.

    O great God, Who art on the throne,
        Give to us the true repentance,
    Give to us the forgiveness of sin, –
        Sin inborn and actual sin.

    Give to us, O God, strong love,
        And that beautiful crown of the King;
    Give us, O God, the home of salvation
        Within the beauteous gates of Thy kingdom.

May Michael, bright warrior of the angels,
    Be keeping the evil enemies down;
May Jesus Christ, the Son of David
    Be giving us hospitality in the brightness of peace.

CG

# Nightfall

## REST BENEDICTION

Bless to me, O God, the moon that is above me,
Bless to me, O God, the earth that is beneath me,
Bless to me, O God, my wife and my children,
And bless, O God, myself who have care of them;
    Bless to me my wife and my children,
    And bless, O God, myself who have care of them.

Bless, O God, the thing on which mine eye doth rest,
Bless, O God, the thing on which my hope doth rest,
Bless, O God, my reason and my purpose,
Bless, O bless Thou them, Thou God of life;
    Bless, O God, my reason and my purpose,
    Bless, O bless Thou them, Thou God of life.

Bless to me the bed-companion of my love,
Bless to me the handling of my hands,
Bless, O bless Thou to me, O God, the fencing of my defence,
And bless, O bless to me the angeling of my rest;
    Bless, O bless Thou to me, O God, the fencing of my defence,
    And bless, O bless to me the angeling of my rest.
    CG

## *Hymn*

*O  AM  GAEL  FFYDD  I  EDRYCH...*

O to have faith to look
with the angels above,
into the plan of salvation.

ANN GRIFFITHS

# The Blessing

The love and affection of the angels be to you,
The love and affection of the saints be to you,
The love and affection of heaven be to you,
    To guard you and to cherish you.

May God shield you on every steep,
May Christ aid you on every path,
May Spirit fill you on every slope,
    On hill and on plain.

CG

# 6 ൦ഉ FRIDAY

*Traditionally dedicated to the Holy Cross
and the Passion of our Lord, Jesus Christ.*

## Morning

### THE PATH OF RIGHT

When the people of the Isles come out in the morning to their tillage, to their fishing, to their farming, or to any of their various occupations anywhere, they say a short prayer called 'Ceum na Còrach', 'The Path of Right', 'The Just or True Way'. If the people feel secure from being overseen or overheard they croon, or sing, or intone their morning prayer in a pleasing musical manner. If, however, any person, and especially if a stranger, is seen in the way, the people hum the prayer in an inaudible undertone peculiar to themselves, like the soft murmur of the ever-murmuring sea, or like the far-distant eerie sighing of the wind among the trees, or like the muffled cadence of far-away waters, rising and falling upon the fitful autumn wind.

My walk this day with God,
My walk this day with Christ,
My walk this day with Spirit,
    The Threefold all-kindly:
    Hò! hò! hò! the Threefold all-kindly.

My shielding this day from ill,
My shielding this night from harm,
Hò! hò! both my soul and my body,
    Be by Father, by Son, by Holy Spirit:
    By Father, by Son, by Holy Spirit.

Be the Father shielding me,
Be the Son shielding me,
Be the Spirit shielding me,
    As Three and as One:
    Hò! hò! hò! as Three and as One.
    CG

# THE LUSTRATION

I am bathing my face
In the mild rays of the sun,
As Mary bathed Christ
In the rich milk of Egypt.

Sweetness be in my mouth,
Wisdom be in my speech,
The love the fair Mary gave her Son
Be in the heart of all flesh for me.

The love of Christ in my breast,
The form of Christ protecting me,
There is not in sea nor on land
That can overcome the King of the Lord's day.

The hand of the Bride about my neck,
The hand of Mary about my breast,
The hand of Michael laving me,
The hand of Christ saving me.

    CG


### Thought for the Day
*Is beò duine an déigh a shàrachadh ach cha bheò e idir an déigh a nàrachadh.*

A man overwhelmed still lives, a man disgraced does not.

### The Consecration of Daily Work

## OCEAN BLESSING

God the Father all-powerful, benign,
Jesu the Son of tears and of sorrow,
With thy co-assistance, O! Holy Spirit.

The Three-One, ever-living, ever-mighty, everlasting,
Who brought the Children of Israel through the Red Sea,
And Jonah to land from the belly of the great creature of the ocean,

Who brought Paul and his companions in the ship,
From the torment of the sea, from the dolour of the waves,
From the gale that was great, from the storm that was heavy.

When the storm poured on the Sea of Galilee,

Sain us and shield and sanctify us,
Be Thou, King of the elements, seated at our helm,
And lead us in peace to the end of our journey.

With winds mild, kindly, benign, pleasant,
Without swirl, without whirl, without eddy,
That would do no harmful deed to us.

We ask all things of Thee, O God,
According to Thine own will and word.

CG

## THE CONSECRATION OF THE SEED

I will go out to sow the seed,
In the name of Him who gave it growth;
I will place my front in the wind,
And throw a gracious handful on high.
Should a grain fall on bare rock,
It shall have no soil in which to grow;
As much as falls into the earth,
The dew will make it to be full.

Friday, day auspicious,
The dew will come down to welcome
Every seed that lay in sleep
Since the coming of cold without mercy;
Every seed will take root in the earth,
As the King of the elements desired,
The braird[1] will come forth with the dew,
It will inhale life from the soft wind.

1.   braird: first sproutings of young grain.

I will come round with my step,
I will go rightways with the sun,
In name of Ariel and the angels nine,
In name of Gabriel and the Apostles kind.
Father, Son, and Spirit Holy,
Be giving growth and kindly substance
To every thing that is in my ground,
Till the day of gladness shall come.

The Feast day of Michael, day beneficent,
I will put my sickle round about
The root of my corn as was wont;
I will lift the first cut quickly;
I will put it three turns round
My head, saying my rune the while,
My back to the airt of the north;
My face to the fair sun of power.

I shall throw the handful far from me,
I shall close my two eyes twice,
Should it fall in one bunch
My stacks will be productive and lasting;
No Carlin will come with bad times
To ask a palm bannock from us,
What time rough storms come with frowns
Nor stint nor hardship shall be on us.

CG

# THE HYMN OF ST PATRICK

I arise today
Through a mighty strength, the invocation of the Trinity,
Through belief in the threeness,
Through confession of the oneness
Of the Creator of Creation.

I arise today
Through the strength of Christ's birth with his baptism,
Through the strength of his crucifixion with his burial,
Through the strength of his resurrection with his ascension,
Through the strength of his descent for the judgement of Doom.

I arise today
Through the strength of the love of the Cherubim,
In the obedience of angels,
In the service of archangels,
In the hope of the resurrection to meet with reward,
In the prayers of patriarchs,
In prediction of prophets,
In preaching of apostles,
In faith of confessors,
In innocence of holy virgins,
In deeds of righteous men.

I arise today
Through the strength of heaven;
Light of sun,
Radiance of moon,
Splendour of fire,
Speed of lightning,
Swiftness of wind,
Depth of sea,
Stability of earth,
Firmness of rock.

I arise today
Through God's strength to pilot me,
God's might to uphold me,
God's wisdom to guide me,
God's eye to look before me,
God's ear to hear me,
God's word to speak to me,
God's hand to guard me,
God's way to lie before me,
God's shield to protect me,
God's host to save me,
From snares of devils,
From temptations of vices,
From everyone who shall wish me ill,
Afar and anear,
Alone and in a multitude.

I summon today all these powers between me and those evils,
Against every cruel merciless power that may oppose my body
and soul,
Against incantations of false prophets,
Against black laws of pagandom,
Against false laws of heretics,
Against craft of idolatry,
Against spells of women and smiths and wizards,
Against every knowledge that corrupts man's body and soul.

Christ to shield me today
Against poisoning, against burning,
Against drowning, against wounding,
So that there come to me abundance of reward.
Christ with me, Christ before me, Christ behind me,
Christ in me, Christ beneath me, Christ above me,
Christ on my right, Christ on my left,
Christ when I lie down, Christ when I sit down, Christ when I arise,
Christ in the heart of every man who thinks of me,
Christ in the mouth of everyone that sees me,
Christ in every ear that hears me.

I arise today
Through a mighty strength, the invocation of the Trinity,
Through belief in the threeness,
Through confession of the oneness
Of the Creator of Creation.

*IRISH* (6TH C.)
(TR. KUNO MEYER)

## CATHOLICITY

He was imprisoned by His Jewish flesh and bones
Within the confines of His country,
But he gave them as living planks to be nailed,
And raised from the grave, despite the guarding,
A catholic body by His Father.

And now Cardiff is as near as Calvary,
Bangor every inch as Bethlehem.
The storms in Cardigan Bay are stilled,
And on each street the deranged
Can obtain salvation at the edge of His hem.

He did not hide his Gospel among the clouds of Judea,
Beyond the eye and tongue of man.
But he gives the life that will last for ever
In a drop of wine and a morsel of bread,
And the Spirit's gift in drops of water.

> *CATHOLIGRWYDD*
> GWENALLT
> (TR. C. DAVIES)

## Thoughts, Pilgrimages and Recollections

### The Community Took Over

At Mass on a Sunday morning in an Irish hillside church, the community took over. Though each individual worshipper was encouraged to contact God directly, all of us nonetheless belonged in communion – literally and figuratively. The mythology, whether Christian or pagan, or that vague and delicious brew of both, led us towards the stability created by belief.

The system brought into play all the five senses – seeing the icons, the altar, the priest; hearing the prayers and hymns; smelling the incense, and even the damp of the Church's fabric; tasting the Communion wafer ... touching the rosary beads, the pew, the kneeler, the altar rails.

Inculcation led towards communal harmony and moral coexistence. But at the basis, as the principal way and means, stood verbal communication. Narrative predominated: all the lessons taken from the higher authority, God or Jesus Christ, were transmitted as legend. Each and every Mass contained a Gospel, frequently a specific retelling of some remarkable event in the life of Christ: between the human and the divine, identification was glimpsed, imitation and aspiration advised.

The Celtic tales re-echoed ...

*THE CELTS*

F. DELANEY

@/@

# Midday

## THE WHITE COW

A widow woman at Tabal, Mull, had a cow ill with the 'tarbhan', swelling from surfeit, and she was wringing her hands and beating her breast to see her beloved cow in pain. At that moment she saw Calum Cille, Columba, and his twelve disciples in their 'curachan', little boat or coracle, rowing home to Iona. The widow ran down to the 'rudha', point, and hailed Calum Cille, and asked him to heal her cow. Calum Cille never turned a dull ear to the poor, to the penitent, to the distressed, and he came ashore and made the 'òra' to the white cow, and the white cow rose upon her feet and shook herself and began to browse upon the green grass before her.

'Go thou home, "brònag", and have faith in the God who made thee and in Christ the Saviour who loved thee and died for thee, and in thine own self, and all will go well with thee and with thy cow.'

Having said this, Calum Cille rejoined his followers in the 'curach' and resumed his journey to Hì.

'Put thou in, O Calum Cille,
    And heal the white cow;
Put thou in, O Calum Cille,
    And heal the cow of water!'

'Put thou in, O Calum Cille,
    And heal the cow beloved;
Put thou in, O Calum Cille,
    And heal my dear cow!'

'How so, O thick-tressed woman,
    Am I to heal thy cow,
My one foot in the coracle,
    My other foot on shore?'

Calum Cille came to the knoll,
    He set his hand on the cow;
He set his one foot in the coracle,
    His other foot on ground.

'I myself break thy swelling,
    I myself kill thine insect,
I lift from thee thy prickliness,
    In the name of the King of the ages!'
    CG

# THE CHARM OF THE TOOTHACHE

The charm placed of Columba
About the right knee of Maol Iodha,
Against pain, against sting, against venom,
    Against tooth disease, against bodily disease.

Said Peter unto James:
'I get no respite from toothache,
But it is with me lying down and rising
    And leaping on my soles.'

Said Christ, answering the problem,
    'The toothache and the rune
Shall not henceforth abide in the same head.'
    CG

# PRAYER FOR PROTECTION

Christ be between me and the fairies,
    My frown upon each tribe of
        them!
This day is Friday on sea and on land –
    My trust, O King, that they shall not hear me.
    CG

## *Wishes, Tales and Longings*

### Christ's Bounties

... O Son of God, do a miracle for me, and change my heart;

Thy having taken flesh to redeem me was more difficult than to transform my wickedness.

It is Thou who, to help me, didst go to be scourged by the Jews;

Thou, dear child of Mary, art the refined molten metal of our forge.

It is Thou who makest the sun bright, together with the ice; it is Thou who createdst the rivers and the salmon all along the river.

That the nut-tree should be flowering, O Christ, it is a rare craft; through Thy skill too comes the kernel, Thou fair ear of our wheat.

Though the children of Eve ill deserve the bird-flocks and the salmon, it was the Immortal One on the cross who made both salmon and birds.

It is He who makes the flower of the sloes grow through the surface of the blackthorn, and the nut-flower on other trees; besides this, what miracle is greater?

TADHG OG O HUIGINN (D. 1448)

(TR. K. H. JACKSON)

### *Passing Thoughts*

*Is mairg a théid do'n traigh 's ha h-eòin fhéin 'ga tréigsinn.*

It is a pity for the one who goes to the shore when the very birds are deserting it.

◎◎

# Evening

MICHAEL OF THE ANGELS

O Michael of the angels
And the righteous in heaven,
Shield thou my soul
    With the shade of thy wing;
Shield thou my soul
    On earth and in heaven;

From foes upon earth,
From foes beneath earth,
From foes in concealment
Protect and encircle
    My soul 'neath thy wing,
        Oh my soul with the shade of thy wing!
    *CG*

## BLESSING OF A HOUSE

Be Christ's cross on your new dwelling,
    Be Christ's cross on your new hearth,
Be Christ's cross on your new abode,
    Upon your new fire blazing.

Be Christ's cross on your topmost grain,
    Be Christ's cross on your fruitful wives,
Be Christ's cross on your virile sons,
    Upon your conceptive daughters.

Be Christ's cross on your means and portion,
    Be Christ's cross on your kin and people,
Be Christ's cross on you each light and darkness,
    Each day and each night of your lives,
    Each day and each night of your lives.

CG

@/@

# Nightfall

## THE CROSS OF CHRIST

Be the cross of Christ between me and the fays
    That move occultly out or in,
Be the cross of Christ between me and all ill,
    And ill will, and ill mishap.

Be the angels of heaven shielding me,
    The angels of heaven this night,
Be the angels of heaven keeping me
    Soul and body alike.

Be the compassing of Christ around me
    From every spectre, from every evil,
From every shame that is coming harmfully
    In darkness, in power to hurt.

Be the compassing of the might of Christ
    Shielding me from every harm,
Be keeping me from everything ruinous
    Coming destructively towards me this night.
    CG

## Hymn

*WRTH GODI'R GROES EI CHYFRI'N GORON...*

Count the cross a crown, and bear it,
cheerful live 'mid all life's woes –
this the Way which, straight though tangled,
to the heavenly city goes.

ANN GRIFFITHS

# The Blessing

May Mary Virgin's Son Himself
Be a generous lamp to you,
To guide you over
The great and awful ocean of eternity.

CG

# 7 &#8286; SATURDAY

*Traditionally dedicated to Mary, the mother of God;*
*God – the Word who became flesh and dwelt among us.*

## Morning

### THE THREE

In name of Father,
In name of Son,
In name of Spirit,
 Three in One:

Father cherish me,
Son cherish me,
Spirit cherish me,
 Three all-kindly.

God make me holy,
Christ make me holy,
Spirit make me holy,
    Three all-holy.

Three aid my hope,
Three aid my love,
Three aid mine eye,
    And my knee from stumbling,
    My knee from stumbling.
    CG


## THE ROCK OF ROCKS

On the Rock of rocks,
The peace of Peter and Paul,
Of James and John the beloved,
And of the pure perfect Virgin,
    The pure perfect Virgin.

The peace of the Father of joy,
The peace of the Christ of pasch,
The peace of the Spirit of grace,
To ourselves and to our children,
    Ourselves and our children.
    CG

### Thought for the Day

*Pan deneuo'r Ysbryd y cynfas gwelwn mai creadigaeth yw'r bydysawd ...*

When the Spirit makes thin the canvas, we see that the universe
    is a creation,
That the worker, because he is a child of God, is a person,
And we see the Christ rising from his cross and Grave like the
    glory of
The Sun in the ailing snow to light up the seventh Heaven.

    GWENALLT
    (TR. CYNTHIA DAVIES)

### The Consecration of Daily Work

## LOOM BLESSING

Bless, O Chief of generous chiefs,
My loom and everything a-near me,
Bless me in my every action,
Make Thou me safe while I live.

From every brownie and fairy woman,
From every evil wish and sorrow,
Help me, O Thou helping Being,
As long as I shall be in the land of the living.

In name of Mary, mild of deeds,
In name of Columba, just and potent,
Consecrate the four posts of my loom,
Till I begin on Monday.

Her pedals, her sleay, and her shuttle,
Her reeds, her warp, and her cogs,
Her cloth-beam, and her thread-beam,
Thrums and the thread of the plies.[1]

Every web,[2] black, white, and fair,
Roan, dun, checked, and red,
Give Thy blessing everywhere,
On every shuttle passing under the thread.

Thus will my loom be unharmed,
Till I shall arise on Monday;
Beauteous Mary will give me of her love,
And there shall be no obstruction I shall not overcome.

CG

1. plies: folds; plaits.
2. web: the weave.

# FISHING BLESSING

On Christmas Day the young men of the townland go out to fish. All the fish they catch are sacred to the widows and the orphans and to the poor, and are distributed among them according to their necessities.

There is a tradition among the people of the Western Isles that Christ required Peter to row 707 strokes straight out from the shore when He commanded him to go and procure the fish containing the tribute-money. Following this tradition, the old men of Uist require the young men to row 707 strokes from the land before casting their lines on Christmas Day. And whatever fish they get are cordially given to the needy as a tribute in the name of Christ, King of the sea, and of Peter, king of fishermen.

The day of light has come upon us,
Christ is born of the Virgin.

In His name I sprinkle the water
Upon every thing within my court.

Thou King of deeds and powers above,
Thy fishing blessing pour down on us.

I will sit me down with an oar in my grasp,
I will row me seven hundred and seven [strokes].

I will cast down my hook,
The first fish which I bring up

In the name of Christ, King of the elements,
The poor shall have it at his wish.

And the king of fishers, the brave Peter,
He will after it give me his blessing.

Ariel, Gabriel and John,
Raphael benign, and Paul,

Columba, tender in every distress,
And Mary fair, the endowed of grace.

Encompass ye us to the fishing-bank of ocean,
And still ye to us the crest of the waves.

Be the King of kings at the end of our course,
Of lengthened life and of lasting happiness.

Be the crown of the King from the Three on high,
Be the cross of Christ adown to shield us.
>    The crown of the King from the Three above,
>    The cross of Christ adown to shield us.
>    CG

## THE CHURCHES

Old ships they are, behind the floodgates
Loitering in the mud and mire;
Rust on their anchor, dirt on their bows,
Their decks without paint and their sails in tatters:
They list as if they have arthritis
In their limbs, not able to get up again:
They have forgotten about the sea except when the floodgate lets
A hint of the tide to them.

They were swept aside by the
Industrial and scientific flood of our world:
There is none of the passion of rebirth under their sails,
Only a thin, comfortable religiosity;
On their masts the banner of the Queen and the regiments,
And the Captain forbidding beer and wine:
Chattering about the Sabbath and the religious organizations
Forgetting man's ecumenical suicide.

If they asked the Breath to raise the floodgates
And ventured out into the unreasonable sea;
The anchor fresh, their sails confident,
Faith on deck, window and door:
They would see the Christ nailed

Technologically on His plutonium Cross;
Descending from it; calming the waters
And stifling the nuclear storms of our age.

*YR EGLWYSI*

GWENALLT

(TR. C. DAVIES)

## Life is Greater than Death

Life is greater than death because it is more alive. To believe that death can lord it over life is the same as believing that non-existence can challenge existence.

And it strikes me that the only difference between non-existence and existence is breath, the breath that creates, the breath that proclaims 'Let there be Light' and the breath which distends the nostrils of man and comes to him from God.

*CUDD FY MEIAU*

PENNAR DAVIES

(TR. C. & S. DAVIES)

# Midday

## CHARM FOR ROSE[3]

See, O Son, the udder,
    Swollen by the rose;
Tell Thou that to Our Lady,
    For 'tis she who bore the Son.

Get thee hence, thou rose,
    Let me see the back of thy feet;
Whole be the udder,
    Drained be the swelling.

Thou rose, dark red and swelling,
    Hard, scabby and foul,
Leave the udder and the breast;
    Reduce the swelling, behold the pap distressed.
    CG

3. Prayer for the healing of a cow

# CHARM FOR CHEST DISEASE

For a cure, they first blew on the finger-tips and then rubbed with the points of the five fingers the front of the shoulder; the 'galar toll' (chest disease) was before and behind the shoulder, 'air chùl agus air bhial na gualainn'.

The hands of God be round thee,
The eye of God be over thee,
The love of the King of the heavens
    Drain from thee thy pang.

Away! away! away!
Dumbly! dumbly! dumbly!
Thy venom be in the ground,
    Thy pain be in the stone!

The arrow which came with fright,
    Salt which heals pain,
The prayer prayed by Jesus Christ,
    To still the fairy arrow.

    CG

### Passing Thoughts

*Ged bu dona as saor bu mhaith a shliseag – nar a thubhairt a bhean an uair a chaochail e.*

Although the carpenter was bad, yet his shavings were good – as his wife said when he died.

# Evening

## PRAYER BEFORE CONFESSION

Jesu, give me forgiveness of sins,
Jesu, keep my guilt in my memory,
Jesu, give me the grace of repentance,
Jesu, give me the grace of forgiveness,
Jesu, give me the grace of submission,
Jesu, give me the grace of earnestness,
Jesu, give me the grace of lowliness,
To make a free confession at this time,
To condemn myself at the chair of confession
Lest I be condemned at the chair of judgment;
Jesu, give me strength and courage
To condemn myself at the chair of confession
Lest I be condemned at the chair of judgment.
It is easier for me to go under subjection for a brief while
Than to go to death during eternity.
Jesu, give me to confess my guilt
As earnestly as were this the moment of my death.

> Jesu, take pity on me,
> Jesu, have mercy on me,
> Jesu, take me to Thee,
> Jesu, aid my soul.

A cause of grief is sin,
     A cause of anguish is death,
A cause of joy is repentance
     And cleansing in the river of health.

୭◎

There will be joy among the angels of heaven
     That I am laved in the pool of confession.

     O my soul, be joyful,
     God is willing to be reconciled to thee,
     Seize His hand while it is stretched out
     To announce to thee a loving reconcilement.

Refuse not Thy hand to me, O my God,
Refuse not Thy hand, O Lord of lords,
For the sake of my Saviour Jesus Christ,
     Let me not go to death everlasting.
     CG

# THE PRAYER OF THE WELL

When a girl goes out at night to the well, she croons a hymn variously called 'Rann Tobair', Rune of the Well; 'Caim Moire', Shelter of Mary; 'Caim Moire Màthar', Shelter of Mary Mother, and by other names. The maiden lilts the rune in the firm belief that the protecting arm of the Mary Mother is shielding her from ill and mishap, natural and supernatural.

The shelter of Mary Mother
Be nigh my hands and my feet
To go out to the well
    And to bring me safely home,
    And to bring me safely home.

May warrior Michael aid me,
May Brigit calm preserve me,
May sweet Brianag give me light,
    And Mary pure be near me,
    And Mary pure be near me.
CG

# Nightfall

## I LIE DOWN THIS NIGHT

I lie down this night with God,
> And God will lie down with me;
I lie down this night with Christ,
> And Christ will lie down with me;
I lie down this night with Spirit,
> And the Spirit will lie down with me;
God and Christ and the Spirit
> Be lying down with me.
>> CG

### *Hymn*

*O AM FYWYD O SANCTEIDDIO
SANCTAIDD ENW PUR FY NUW.*

O to spend my whole life
sanctifying the holy name of my God.
> ANN GRIFFITHS

◎◎

# The Blessing

May the blessing of light
be on you, light without and light within.
May the blessed sunlight
shine upon you and warm your heart till it glows
like a great peat fire, so that the stranger may
come and warm himself at it, as well as the friend.
And may the light shine out of the eyes of you,
like a candle set in the windows of a house,
bidding the wanderer to come in out of the storm.
And may the blessing of the rain
be on you – the soft sweet rain.
May it fall upon your spirit so that all the little flowers may spring up,
and shed their sweetness on the air.
And may the blessing of the great rains be on you,
that they beat upon your spirit and wash it fair and clean,
and leave there many a shining pool where the blue
of heaven shines, and sometimes a star.
And may the blessing of the earth
be on you – the great round earth;
may you ever have a kindly greeting
for people you pass as you are going along the roads.
And now may the Lord
bless you, and bless you kindly.

*CYDYMAITH Y PERERIN*

AN OLD IRISH BLESSING

(TR. B. O'MALLEY)

# BIBLIOGRAPHY

## Principal Sources

Bowen, E., *Euros Bowen – Priest/Poet*, Church in Wales Publications, Cardiff, 1993.

Carmichael, A., *Carmina Gadelica* (vol. 1, 1900; vol. 2, 1900; vol. 3, 1940; vol. 4, 1941; vol. 5, 1954; vol. 6, 1971), Scottish Academic Press, Edinburgh.

Clancy, J. P., (ed.), *20th Century Welsh Poems*, Gomer, Llandysul, 1982.

Delaney, F., *The Celts*, Grafton, London, 1989.

Jackson, K. H., (trans.), *A Celtic Miscellany*, Routledge & Kegan Paul, London, 1951.

Mackechnie, *Gaelic Without Groans*, Addison Wesley Longman, Harlow.

O'Malley, B., *Cydymaith y Pererin*, Gomer, Llandysul, 1989.

## General Reading

Bede, *History of the English Church and People*, tr. L. Shirley-Price, Penguin, London, 1955.

Campbell, J., *The Power of Myth*, Doubleday, New York, 1988.

de Mello, A., *Awareness*, Fount, London, 1990.

de Waal, E., (ed.), *The Celtic Vision*, Darton, Longman & Todd, London, 1988.

Delaney, F., *Legends of the Celts*, Grafton, London, 1989.

Duncan, A., *The Elements of Celtic Christianity*, Element, Shaftesbury, 1992.

Evans, K. M., *A Book of Welsh Saints*, Church in Wales Publications,
Cardiff, 1967.

Farmer, D. H., *The Oxford Dictionary of Saints*, Clarendon, Oxford, 1978.

Foster, R. F., *Modern Ireland 1600 – 1972*, Penguin, London, 1989.

Fox, M., *Original Blessing*, Bear & Co., Santa Fe, USA, 1983.

Herm, G., *The Celts*, Weidenfeld, London, 1976.

Jones, G., (ed.), *The Oxford Book of Welsh Verse in English*, Oxford University
Press, Oxford, 1977.

Kinsella, T., (tr.), *The Oxford Book of Irish Verse*, Oxford University Press,
Oxford, 1986; *Tain Bo Cuailnge*, Oxford University Press, Oxford, 1970.

Mac Eacharna, D., *The Lands of Lordship*, Argyll Reproductions, 1976.

Mackie, J. D., *A History of Scotland*, Pelican, London, 1964.

Maclean, G. R. D., *Praying with Highland Christians*, Triangle/SPCK,
London, 1988.

Marsden, J., *The Illustrated Colmcille*, Macmillan, London, 1991.

Matthews, C., *The Elements of the Celtic Tradition*, Element, Shaftesbury, 1989.

Meyer, K., (ed.), *Selections from Ancient Irish Poetry*, Constable, London, 1959.

O'Donnell, M., (ed.), *Betha Colaim Chille*, A. O'Kellehar & G. Schoepperle,
1918.

Scott, A. B., *The Pictish Nation: its People and its Church*, Foulis,
Edinburgh, 1918.

Thomas, C., *Celtic Britain*, Thames & Hudson, London, 1986.

Thomas, Patrick, *Candle in the Darkness*, Gomer, Llandysul, 1993.

Tunney, J., *St Colmcille and the Columban Heritage*, St Colmcille Heritage
Trust, 1987.

# ACKNOWLEDGEMENTS

The poem 'A Celtic Christ' (page 45) is reproduced by kind permission of its author, M. T. Harris.

The poems of Euros Bowen from *Euros Bowen – Priest/Poet*, © Church in Wales Publications, 1993, are reproduced by permission of the publishers.

The poems of Gwenallt are published by permission of Gwasg Gomer, Llandysul, Ceredigion.

The hymn-verses (in translation) of Ann Griffiths, the meditation of the Resurrection and an extract from *Cudd Fy Meiau* by Pennar Davies, the translations by C. & S. Davies of Meirion Davies' 'Credaf' and Donald Evans' 'Crist Natur', and a number of traditional blessings and sayings are all reproduced from *A Welsh Pilgrim's Manual*, edited by Rev. Brendan O'Malley, with his kind permission and that of the publishers, Gwasg Gomer.

The translations of original Celtic material taken from *A Celtic Miscellany*, by the late Kenneth Hurlstone Jackson, are reproduced by kind permission of his widow and of the publishers, Routledge.

The author and publisher would particularly like to thank the trustees of the *Carmina Gadelica*, for their permission to reproduce several extracts from the six volumes; also to Dr Douglas Grant from the Scottish Academic Press, for his invaluable help in ensuring that the extracts were sourced and reproduced correctly. The references for each extract used are as follows:

## Sunday

The Guiding Light of Eternity: vol. 1, p. 33.
The Cross of the Saints and the Angels: vol. 1, p. 47.
Kindling the Fire: vol. 1, p. 233.
Milking Croon: vol. 1, p. 259.
Hymn of the Sunday: vol. 1, p. 223.
Prayer at Dressing: vol. 3, p. 25.
Sain for Sheep: vol. 4, p. 49.
A Blessing for Health and Healing/Charm: vol. 4, p. 313.
Birth Baptism: vol. 3, pp. 7–9.
Peace: vol. 3, p. 265.
Smooring the Fire: vol. 3, p. 327.

## Monday

Prayer at Rising: vol. 3, p. 29.
Invocation for Justice: vol. 1, p. 53.
Herding Blessing: vol. 1, p. 277.
Hunting Blessing: vol. 1, pp. 310–13.

Driving the Cows: vol. 4, pp. 40–41.

Charm for the Evil Eye: vol. 4, p. 171.

The Sun: vol. 3, pp. 306–307.

The Baptism by the Knee-woman: vol. 3, pp. 17–19.

The Homestead: vol. 3, p. 359.

Blessing: vol. 3, p. 211.

## Tuesday

Prayer at Dressing: vol. 3, pp. 25–27.

Desires: vol. 1, p. 51.

Reaping Blessing: vol. 1, p. 249.

Charm of the Butter: vol. 4, p. 85.

Kidney of Mary: vol. 4, p. 193.

Death: vol. 3, pp. 379–381.

The Mother's Parting Blessing: vol. 3, pp. 246–9.

Encompassing of Family: vol. 3, p. 355.

Blessing: vol. 3, p. 211.

## Wednesday

Thanksgiving: vol. 3, p. 31.

Come I This Day: vol. 1, p. 69.

Loom Blessing: vol. 1, p. 301.

The Blessing of the Parching: vol. 1, pp. 250–251.

Prayer of the Teats: vol. 4, pp. 62–3.

Charm for Chest Seizure: vol. 4, pp. 249–253.

The New Moon: vol. 3, p. 305.

Petition: vol. 3, p. 171.

Sleep Invocation: vol. 3, p. 335.

Blessing: vol. 3, p. 211.

## Thursday

Prayer at Rising: vol. 3, p. 33.

Prayer for Victory: vol. 1, p. 57.

The Chant of the Warping: vol. 1, pp. 295–9.

Clipping Blessing: vol. 1, p. 293.

Columba's Herding: vol. 4, p. 47.

Charm for Consumption: vol. 4, p. 265.

The Virgin: vol. 3, p. 115.

A Prayer for a Joyous Death: vol. 3, p. 387.

Rest Benediction: vol. 3, p. 339.

Blessing: vol. 3, p. 339.

## Friday

The Path of Right: vol. 3, pp. 48–9.

The Lustration: vol. 1, p. 59.

Ocean Blessing: vol. 1, p. 329.

The Consecration of the Seed: vol. 1, pp. 243–5.

The White Cow: vol. 4, pp. 288–91.

The Charm of the Toothache: vol. 4, p. 199.

Prayer for Protection: vol. 5, p. 251.

Michael of the Angels: vol. 3, p. 149.

Blessing of a House: vol. 3, p. 367.

The Cross of Christ: vol. 3, p. 263.

Blessing: vol. 3, p. 205.

## Saturday

The Three: vol. 3, p. 63.

The Rock of Rocks: vol. 1, p. 43.

Loom Blessing: vol. 1, p. 305.

Fishing Blessing: vol. 1, pp. 318–321.

Charm for Rose: vol. 4, p. 189.

Charm for Chest Disease: vol. 4, pp. 306–307.

Prayer Before Confession: vol. 3, pp. 257–9.

The Prayer of the Well: vol. 3, pp. 168–169.

I Lie Down This Night: vol. 3, p. 333.

# INDEX

# CELTIC JOURNEYS

## Shirley Toulson

As interest grows in Britain's Celtic heritage, Shirley Toulson's book provides an easy guide to the places associated with its remarkable teachers and missionaries – the Celtic Saints.

*Celtic Journeys* contains eight tours in Scotland and the North of England, each based upon the movements of specific individuals and their followers. They include Ninian, Kentigern, Columba, Kenneth, Adomnan, Cuthbert, Aidan and Hilda.

With informative maps to accompany the tours, this beautiful book will help the traveller to understand the way in which the Celtic Saints turned their backs on the dark centuries that preceded their emergence, bringing the light of learning and of faith to the barbarous tribes of England and Scotland.

# CELTIC DAILY PRAYER

## From the Northumbria Community

> Christ as a light
> Illumine and guide me
> Christ as a shield
> O'ershadow me...
> Christ as a light
> Christ as a shield
> Christ beside me
> On my left and my right.

The ancient and beautiful tradition of daily prayer finds new expression in this collection of readings shaped by Celtic spirituality.

Morning, midday and evening prayers, meditations, an order for Holy Communion, a Family Shabbat and a reading for every day of the year are all included in this treasury of Celtic material to be used time and time again.

# CELTIC NIGHT PRAYER

## From the Northumbria Community

*Celtic Night Prayer* is the accompanying volume to *Celtic Daily Prayer*,
compiled by members of the Northumbria Community. This
beautiful book comprises simple complines for each day of the week,
together with special liturgies for various feasts of the Christian year
and a reading for every day of the year.

When night closes in, we have to look at things differently.
There are many sorts of night – the long nights of winter time,
nights of difficulty or unanswered questions, times of loneliness and
the apparent absence of God. There is also the warmth of time spent
with friends, the happy tiredness at the end of the day, the joy of the
bridal night or thanksgiving at an evening meal.

The Celtic understanding welcomes and celebrates the presence
of Christ in all of these.

Be with us, Lord.
We have joy, we have joy.
When I awake,
I am still with you.

# A LITTLE BOOK OF COMFORT

*An anthology of grief and love*

## Anthony Guest

Grief is never mild. In its early, intense stages it threatens to overwhelm and extinguish all hope. This has been the experience of men and women down the centuries, in all cultures. But so too has the healing which follows. Slow, imperceptible, yet inevitable, it is a personal affirmation we each receive of the triumph of life over death and the indestructibility of love.

From Dante and Shakespeare to Emily Brontë, Robert Graves and C. S. Lewis, this anthology draws together a selection of the most moving, comforting and inspiring writings of all time on the themes of loss and love.

# LAUGHTER, SILENCE AND SHOUTING

*An anthology of women's prayers*

## Compiled by Kathy Keay

*Laughter, Silence and Shouting* is a wide-ranging anthology of prayers that articulate women's deepest longings, fears, joys and dreams. Included are prayers by Mother Teresa, Florence Nightingale, Emily Brontë, Helen Keller, Janet Morley, Teresa of Avila and Julian of Norwich.

Ranging in origin from the Celtic tradition to modern day feminist theologians, these prayers offer gentle spiritual guidance and introspection for women everywhere. Over 160 prayers are presented in categories such as 'Our Daily Lives', 'Relationships', 'Work', 'Illness', 'Grief', 'Daring to Believe', 'Stages of Life', and many more.

This beautiful book is the perfect gift for reflection and meditation, and provides a useful resource for women the world over.

# DANCING ON MOUNTAINS
*An anthology of women's spiritual writings*

## Compiled by Kathy Keay

'I have named this anthology Dancing On Mountains, for in the midst of
life's demands, there are always moments to celebrate; historic and often
incidental moments of breakthrough, breathtaking, inspiring and energizing,
when the Spirit enlivens the commonplace, making us want to dance.'
KATHY KEAY

*Dancing On Mountains* is a collection of writing by women of all ages,
times, conditions and countries, expressing their spirituality, through
their everyday lives and through the unbridled possibilities of their
dreams. Including selections from Emily Brontë, Helen Keller and
Emily Dickinson, as well as many previously unknown writers, each
passage in *Dancing On Mountains* reflects a voice which will inspire,
encourage, and comfort readers on their own journey through life.

After reading English at Oxford, Kathy Keay worked as a
freelance writer, editor and journalist, giving workshops and seminars
in the UK, the USA, India, Africa and South Africa. Kathy was a
prolific writer, with nine published titles to her credit. She died in
December 1994, after a long fight against cancer.